Successful Credit Control

in a week

ROGER MASON

Hodder & Stoughton

A MEMBER OF THE HODDER HEADLINE GROUP

Orders: please contact Bookpoint Ltd, 39 Milton Park, Abingdon, Oxon OX14 4TD. Telephone: (44) 01235 400414, Fax: (44) 01235 400454. Lines are open from 9.00 - 6.00, Monday to Saturday, with a 24 hour message answering service. Email address: orders@bookpoint.co.uk

British Library Cataloguing in Publication Data
A catalogue record for this title is available from The British Library

ISBN 0 340 74752 X

First published 1999

Impression number	10	9	8	7	6	5	4	3	2	1
Year	2005	2004	2003	2002	2001	2000	1999			

Cover photo from TCL Stock Directory UK
Typeset by Multiplex Techniques Ltd, St Mary Cray, Kent.
Printed in Great Britain for Hodder & Stoughton Educational, a division of Hodder Headline Plc, 338 Euston Road, London NW1 3BH by Cox & Wyman Ltd, Reading, Berkshire.

the Institute of Management

FOUNDATION

The mission of the Institute of Management (IM) is to promote the art and science of management.

The Institute embraces all levels of management from student to chief executive and supports its own Foundation which provides a unique portfolio of services for all managers, enabling them to develop skills and achieve management excellence.

For information on the various levels and benefits of membership, please contact:

Department HS
Institute of Management
Cottingham Road
Corby
Northants NN17 1TT
Tel: 01536 204222
Fax: 01536 201651

This series is commissioned by the Institute of Management Foundation.

C O N T E N T S

There is an excellent training film with the title *Who Killed the Sale?* Many managers have seen it and will recall that the answer to the question is that they all did. Perhaps one day someone will make a training film called *Who Killed the Cash Flow?* The message would be very similar because good credit control, like sales, should be everyone's business.

Credit control sometimes does not get the priority that it deserves. It is always important and can sometimes make the difference between a profit and a loss. In extreme cases, poor cash flow and bad debts can threaten the survival of a business. That concerns everyone, or should do.

This book is written for managers wishing to improve their knowledge of this vital subject. By putting aside a little time each day for a week, you should master the basics in many areas and lay the foundations for future effectiveness.

Everyone associated with this book wishes you success in practising what you will learn.

Here is our plan for the week:

Sunday	Opening a new account
Monday	The effective use of letters
Tuesday	The effective use of the telephone
Wednesday	Dealing with excuses
Thursday	Other collection methods and interest
Friday	Sources of information and signs of trouble
Saturday	The end of the line: legal action

Opening a new account

Today we start at the beginning and look at the things that must be done, or at least thought about, when a new account is opened. The points for consideration are:

- Application for a credit account
- References
- Credit limits
- Fixing the terms

What you do, or do not do, when you open a new credit account will send a message to your new customer. He may not realise that this message has been sent, but it will probably influence his future behaviour. Perhaps nothing at all will happen when you open a new credit account. This sends a strong message to the customer, and it is not one that you want him to receive. To do nothing is a mistake, and it is a mistake that is frequently made.

Your new customer should realise that you have the virtues of the three Fs. You should be firm, fair and friendly. When a new account is opened, you will want to achieve three things:

1 obtain all the information that you need;
2 make sensible decisions about credit and terms;
3 agree the terms of business with the customer, and make sure that he understands the way that you intend the account to be operated.

Most customers will respect a firm, fair and friendly approach and will respond in a positive way. Some will not,

and this is valuable information for you. If there are going to be problems, it is best to know right at the beginning. Then you can control the situation and not let a crisis develop. It might even be necessary to refuse credit altogether.

Do not overlook the importance of getting full, accurate information. You are much more likely to be paid swiftly if the customer receives prompt and accurate invoices, statements and other documents. You can only do this if you have obtained the right details, and this is best done when a new account is opened.

Application for a credit account

It may be possible to obtain all the information by an exchange of letters, and the terms of business may be fixed in the same way. However, it is very often a good idea to get the new customer to fill in a form. This can be designed to reveal all the information that you want.

You should design a form that suits your business, but the next page contains an example of a good all-purpose form. This achieves quite a lot. For a start it gives the exact name and address of the buyer. Both will be needed for invoices and statements as well as for contract purposes. This is important. Ann Brown is not the same as Ann Brown Ltd, even if she owns the company, places the orders and lives on the premises.

The form gives an indication of the amount of credit that the customer anticipates needing. This will influence your decisions in setting a credit limit, and it may influence your judgment about the extent to which references should be checked. The form gives two references and authorises you to approach them.

Most importantly, the form states that the conditions of sale have been read and agreed, and that invoices are payable within 30 days. Just printing the terms on invoices and statements does not legally commit the buyer. They must be agreed before or at the time that the contract is made. Furthermore, the person signing the form is more likely to feel a moral commitment, which is exactly what you want to happen. You will later be able to quote a name and a signed agreement if necessary.

An application form should contain the following:

- exact details of name and address
- details of references (if required)
- a legal and moral commitment to accept the terms of business, especially the period of credit
- a signature

An example of a good application form for a credit account

To: **Levy Catering Supplies Ltd**
129 Cowley Street
Oxford

Dear Sir

We request you to open a credit account in the name of:

....

Address ....

....

We accept that all invoices are payable within 30 days of date of issue. We have read your standard conditions of sale and agree that they will govern all trading between us. The maximum amount of credit required is expected to be £...

Details of two trade referees are given below and we authorise you to make the normal enquiries of them.

Signature ....

Name ....

Position................................

Referee 1	Referee 2
Name	Name...................................
Address	Address..................................
....	....

References

A customer in trouble may pay just a few accounts promptly in order to ensure a supply of good references. Even worse, a customer might give an accommodation address and write his own. Despite these possibilities, cheating is relatively rare, and trade references are often a source of very useful information.

The taking of references has become more common, and for good reasons. They do help. You should make it as easy as possible for the person writing a reference. It is a good idea to send a pre-printed form that can be completed quickly, together with a stamped addressed envelope. This will increase your chances of getting a reply.

It is surprisingly common for a person to ask for a reference, then ignore a bad reply or no reply. This is silly, and if you are going to do this you might as well not bother to ask. At the very least, you should seek further references. If you get no reply at all, you should follow up with a telephone call.

An example of a good letter requesting a trade reference is shown on the next page.

An example of a good request for a trade reference

PRIVATE AND CONFIDENTIAL

Dear Sir

K.R. Cohen Ltd of 77 Hillside Close, Exeter

The above has given your name as a trade reference. We would be grateful if you would answer the questions at the foot of this letter and return it in the enclosed prepaid envelope.

Your reply will be treated in strict confidence, and at any time we will be pleased to respond to a similar request from yourselves.

Yours faithfully

Sharon Smith
Credit Controller

How long has the above-named traded with you? ....

What is the highest credit allowed? £.......................................

What are your payment terms?

....

Is payment normally Prompt/Slow/Very Slow

Do you recommend them for total credit of £..........? Yes/No

Any other information that you think might be helpful.

....

....

Credit limits

When you have opened an account, your new customer is able to trade on credit and expose you to risk. It is often sensible to limit this risk by fixing a credit limit. Of course, a credit limit may be revised later when you have better information and the experience of running the account. There are three good reasons for setting a credit limit:

1 It is a very effective way of limiting the risk.
2 Only modest checks have been done, or perhaps no checks at all.
3 Checks have been done and they reveal something worrying.

There is a limit to how much time and money it is sensible to spend on references and other checks, especially if it is likely to be a small account. A credit limit is a way of taking the risk but capping the possible damage. The same applies to an account where there is cause for concern. You probably want the business – after all, profits are earned from accounts that are opened, not from accounts that are not opened. If a limit of say £1,000 is set, provided that it is properly enforced, you cannot lose more than £1,000. This might be a sensible compromise.

You may or may not choose to tell the customer what the limit is, but it is usually best to do so. It is only fair and he might be able to give you more information that will persuade you to increase it. He will find out anyway if it results in an order being refused.

A further reason for credit limits is that they can restrict losses caused by fraud or a sudden worsening of a customer's position. A customer in trouble may want to increase the level of business. This is normally good news, but not if it is because he cannot get supplies elsewhere. Take for example an account with a limit of £10,000 which has in the past been adequate. Then a sudden order for £20,000 is placed. This may be good business, but it may be a fraud or it may be placed because other suppliers are refusing credit. Without a credit limit, the order would probably be fulfilled without question. After all, it is a good order, and the account might not even be in arrears. A credit limit forces you to think. There may be excellent reasons for overriding the limit, but it must be a conscious decision and cannot go through by default.

Fixing the terms

The most important of the terms is the one that fixes the
period of credit. There are three very good reasons for
making it as short as possible:

1 It is obviously in your interests to be paid quickly.
2 A few customers will pay to terms – whatever they are.
3 More customers will pay a set number of days past the
   due settlement date – whatever it is.

Do keep in mind that a fixed number of days is preferable
to a term such as 'monthly account', which means the end
of the month following the invoice date. This is 45 days on
average.

The period of credit is only one of the conditions of sale,
though it is often the most important. There may be many
others, including all those that have no connection with
payment or credit control. The method of payment is one
that does. This may be particularly important in the case of
export sales, and you may, for example, want to specify
that payment must be to a UK bank in sterling.

Another important possible condition is the opportunity to
take settlement discount for prompt payment. You may say,
for example: '30 days or 5% settlement discount for payment
within 7 days.' This can be effective in persuading customers
to pay quickly, but it is essential that it be effectively
controlled. Some customers will try to deduct it without
paying in the permitted time. It may also be expensive. The
above example is equivalent to 79 per cent per annum.

It is not practical to put all the terms on the front of the credit application form. It is usual either to put them on the back or to make them available separately.

The exception to this should be the period of credit, which should appear prominently on the front. This is because the customer should know what is required, and should be morally committed as well as legally committed. You may need to remind him later of what was agreed and perhaps send him a copy of the form containing his signature.

It may be difficult to ensure that your conditions are legally binding. The customer may have his own conditions. They may stipulate a long payment period, and there may be other terms that you do not like. He may refuse to sign the form and insist that his purchase conditions apply. He may even ask you to sign these. Whether or not the seller backs down, or insists on the seller's conditions, must in the end be a matter of commercial judgment.

It sometimes happens that neither side is willing to concede, and you should be aware of the legal consequences when this happens. The position when the contract is made is what counts. What happens or is said afterwards does not matter. So the last letter, or the last thing that is said, will usually decide whose terms apply. It can get very childish, but you need to be sure that your letter is the last one before the order is placed and accepted.

Summary and checklist

Today is well summed up by the following checklist. You should tick each item to show that you understand its

importance. The last point sums up good business practice as well as good credit control. It pays to be firm, fair and friendly.

- Do something. The absolute minimum is to write and confirm the terms.
- If there are going to be problems, now is the best time to find out.
- Be sure to get full, factual information.
- An application-for-credit form is often a good idea.
- Such a form should state the period of credit prominently on the front.

- Your conditions of sale will only apply if they are accepted, or last on the table, when a contract is made. An application-for-credit form should achieve this.
- References are useful in most cases.
- A bad reference should not be ignored, and neither should a failure to reply be ignored.
- Credit limits cap your exposure. They are often a good idea.
- The period of credit is often the most important of the conditions.
- At all times, you should be firm, fair and friendly. This is good credit control, and it is good business practice.

The effective use of letters

Letters and telephone calls are the two most common methods of credit control. Telephone calls generally produce better results, but, for many businesses, letters are an essential method of collection. They do have disadvantages, which are mentioned shortly, and it is up to you to minimise these and send out strong, effective requests for payment that get the money in. Computers and modern technology help a lot, but you must not forget the principles of good letter writing. Today's programme is:

- Advantages of letters
- Disadvantages of letters
- Standard letters
- The final warning letter
- Effective individual letters

Advantages of letters

The obvious advantage is that it is relatively cheap to send out a large number of standard letters. Provided that your sales ledger data is in good order, and provided that you take advantage of modern technology, it is a cost-effective way of chasing payment. So long as standard letters are well-designed and well-produced, they can convey an effective message. An individually written letter is of course better, but much more expensive to produce.

Some customers like to have a piece of paper as a reminder. They may use it to check their accounts-payable information, and some will not make a payment unless they receive a letter or statement. This is very unfair, but such customers do exist. It is in your interests to see that these customers receive a reminder letter very early in the collection process.

A further advantage is that complicated figures and information can be included in a letter, or attached to it. This is not possible with a telephone call. Such information may be very helpful to a customer who is willing to pay but is having a problem with the account.

A reminder letter may be less embarrassing to receive than a telephone call. Admittedly, some customers are almost impossible to embarrass, and you might want to do it anyway. Nevertheless, it usually pays to keep on good terms with your customers, even the problem ones. So a friendly letter does have advantages.

Finally, a letter is a permanent record, so long as it is not thrown away of course. This is important when you face serious problems, and the final warning before legal action should be in the form of a letter.

Disadvantages of letters

You should realise that a certain number of the letters that you write will go straight into the bin. This will be so even if they are short, well-written and well-presented, and is because it is what some customers do to letters asking for payment. You should of course still write letters that are short, well-written and well-presented. This will reduce the failure rate and improve the overall results.

One of the advantages of letters is that they are a permanent record, but this is only an advantage if you get it right. If you make a mistake, a letter is a permanent record of it, which is the last thing that you want. However, this should not be a serious problem to you.

The major disadvantage of letters is that there is no personal contact. You cannot look the other person in the eye, and you do not have the chance to hear a human voice. You cannot get a reaction, discuss any problems and hopefully solve them on the spot. You cannot make an assessment of what is said and the tone of voice used. The printed word is less likely than the spoken word to persuade a slow payer.

Standard letters

The use of standard letters is almost inevitable when there are a large number of individually small debts to collect. The red reminders sent out by telephone and electricity companies are very effective examples of standard letters, though these utilities are greatly assisted by customers' fears of the sanction of being disconnected.

It may well not be a good idea to have more than one standard letter before moving to the final warning letter. Individual cases vary, and you must use your judgment. If there is a second letter, the wording should make it clear that it is not the first. It will be more likely to be ignored if the customer thinks that it is the first letter. Whatever the system, it is a good idea to vary it from time to time. Customers may get to anticipate the letters and know for how long they can safely be ignored.

Whatever the system of standard letters, it will pay to start early. There is nothing to be gained by waiting, and the earlier that you ask, the earlier that you are likely to be paid.

Standard letters are most likely to achieve good results if
the following rules are observed:

- Letters should be individually signed if possible,
  even if they have been produced en masse. This
  increases the likely impact.
- Letters should be short. Long letters are much more
  likely to be disregarded.
- An effort should be made to personalise each letter
  and disguise the fact that it is mass produced.
- The tone should always be polite but firm. Never
  apologise for asking for an overdue payment.
- Customers should be given an opportunity to raise
  queries.
- Letters should look impressive. They should be well-
  printed on good-quality paper.
- If possible, letters should be addressed to a named
  person.
- Letters should not include phrases such as 'Please
  ignore this letter if payment has been made
  recently.' It is unnecessary and looks weak.
- The database must be kept up to date. Customers
  will be infuriated if the same mistakes are repeated
  time after time.

The next page shows an example of a good first standard
letter. Note that it is addressed to a named person and that the
tone is polite but firm. There is an opportunity to raise
queries.

An example of a good first standard letter

R. Lloyd Esq.
Chief Accountant
Lambeth and Crystal Ltd
47 Church Square
Gloucester

1 September 1999

Dear Mr Lloyd

We notice that a balance of £911.21 is overdue for payment. We are not aware of any reason why payment should not be made, but please do let me have details if this is the case.

If your payment is on the way to us, please accept our thanks. Otherwise could we please have your remittance by return.

Yours sincerely

Sharon O'Reilly
Credit Controller

The final warning letter

The final communication before legal action is commenced should almost always be in the form of a letter. A good final warning letter that is clear, firm, credible and unambiguous will achieve early payment in more than half of all cases. It is therefore worth taking trouble to make this a very good letter. By definition, there is only one final warning letter. There is something wrong if you send more than one, and the customer is not likely to be impressed. A good final warning letter contains the following features:

- It should not contain empty threats. If you do not mean it, do not say it.
- Like other letters, and despite the purpose, it should be polite but firm. Do not be abusive.
- The letter should state exactly what will happen if payment is not made by the stated date. There should be no ambiguity.
- The letter should be short and to the point.
- It is often a good idea to address the letter to the Company Secretary or some such person, with a copy going to the original contact. This increases the impact of the letter.
- It is a good idea to send the letter by recorded delivery. This is to increase the impact, and does not imply criticism of the postal authorities.

A good example of a final warning letter appears on the following page. It contains all the above features.

An example of a good final warning letter

The Company Secretary
Lambeth and Crystal Ltd
47 Church Square
Gloucester

20 September 1999

Dear Sir

Overdue Balance of £911.21

We notice with regret that the above balance is still outstanding. Although we wrote on 1 September and 10 September, we have received neither payment nor a reason why payment should not be made.

We must now tell you that we expect payment to be made by 27 September. If payment has not been received by that date, we will pass the matter to our solicitors with instructions to commence legal proceedings. This will be done without further warning to you.

Yours sincerely

Sharon O'Reilly
Credit Controller

cc   R. Lloyd Esq.

Effective individual letters

An effective individual letter will incorporate the good points of an effective standard letter. It is worth looking back to see what these are. To make the point again, an individual letter will make more impact if it is well-produced on good-quality paper. This is true of invoices and statements as well.

You may write a letter because you have a lot of complicated information to convey. Nevertheless, a long, complicated letter may not receive the attention that it deserves. You must therefore take steps to make it as easy to follow as possible. Perhaps the points should be numbered. Perhaps it should be a short letter that makes the main points, and with the complicated figures on attached sheets.

An individually composed letter is expensive and time-consuming, so you must make it count. You have the opportunity to write a really personal missive, perhaps something that is a pleasure to receive, even though it does ask for money. You can express yourself, use well-chosen phrases and, above all, relate it to the person who will receive it. It is a personal letter, so make it personal.

Humour is often effective in credit control, and this is true of letter writing. It helps if you know the customer and know what can safely be said. You might, for example, after receipt of an unexpectedly small sum, write thanking a customer for the down payment and asking for the remainder. You could say that your money-lending licence has not come through and that you have to be paid. The cartoons in this book may give you ideas.

Summary

Today we have:

- seen the advantages of letters and how to make the most of these advantages
- seen the disadvantages and how to minimise them
- seen when to use standard letters and how to make them as effective as possible
- seen how to write a telling final warning letter
- seen three good sample letters
- looked at how to write good individual letters, and especially at how to make them personal

Letters and telephone calls are the two main methods of collection. Tomorrow we will look at the effective use of the telephone.

The effective use of the telephone

Tuesday is a solid working day towards the middle of the week. It is a good day to study a solid, very effective method of collecting outstanding debts. Many, perhaps most, credit controllers find that mastery of telephone collection is the most important part of their job. It is a skill that must not be neglected. Our programme today is as follows:

- Advantages of telephone collection
- Disadvantages of telephone collection
- The right attitude
- Preparation for the call
- How to reach the right person
- A successful call
- The conclusion

Advantages of telephone collection

There are a lot of advantages, and telephone calls are often effective when used to follow up standard letters. For a start, they are not expensive in money terms. Telephone calls get cheaper each year, both in relative terms and often in absolute terms too. Modern technology is available to help credit controllers who need to make a lot of calls. Services such as ringback and automatic database dialling increase the number of calls that can be made in a given time. Modern computer systems allow relevant account details to be displayed on a desktop screen as each call is made.

The main advantage of a telephone call is that personal contact is established with a customer. It is this that ensures that many credit controllers find that, next to personal visits, it is the most effective method of collection. The caller can hold a conversation, listen to points made by the customer and in many cases give an on-the-spot response. It is a two-way process, and this has great advantages.

A telephone call puts moral pressure on the person receiving it. It is difficult to ignore, and many will feel a need to honour a commitment. Penetrating questions, even though asked in a friendly way, help to achieve this. In yesterday's chapter, it was stated that letters are less likely to embarrass a customer. But in some cases you do want to embarrass a customer, even if most times it is only mild embarrassment. An embarrassed customer who respects the caller is likely to make prompt payment.

Disadvantages of telephone collection

Perhaps the biggest disadvantage is that calls are relatively time-consuming. You cannot just contact a thousand customers in the way that you can send out a thousand standard letters.

It may be difficult to reach the right person, and so repeated calls may be necessary. Customers are often busy people, and many really do spend a lot of time in meetings. This is not always an excuse. Telephone technology can work against you as well as help you. More and more customers are choosing to hide behind recorded messages, music, multiple-choice options etc. A customer may screen his calls with voicemail and decide later who he wants to ring back. Someone asking for money may not be high on the list.

It is difficult to give complicated details on the phone. You can really only convey a message such as 'You owe me a lot of money, and payment is late. Please can I have a cheque straight away.' Admittedly this is an excellent message to convey, and it is a big achievement to get it across, but you might have to sort out some details afterwards. There is no permanent record of a telephone conversation.

The right attitude

Many people dislike making telephone calls with the purpose of asking for payment. They may be shy and embarrassed or just not like it. They may fear rudeness or feel that a lack of telephone skills will make it an unenjoyable experience. Such people may seek to avoid making calls or prepare so much that little time is left for the actual calls. This is understandable, but it is not justified and it is completely the wrong attitude.

You have every right to ask for money that is owing. If anyone should be nervous, it is the person that you are ringing. Keep telling yourself this. It is the truth.

Even if you are not brilliant on the telephone, you can tell yourself that there are a lot of rewards for hard work and making a lot of calls. Perhaps your less-than-perfect approach will achieve early payment from 60 per cent of the customers that you ring. If you make 100 calls, you will do just as well as someone who gets 75 per cent from 80 calls. Of course, it is even better to get 75 per cent from 100 calls, and you probably can. You are likely to be your harshest critic, so, to use the modern phrase, 'Just go for it.'

It will help your confidence and your success rate if you prepare properly. Do the preparation, but do not put off making the calls. Just pick up the telephone and start ringing. Be persistent, and generally be friendly but firm, and tough if necessary. Tell yourself that you are on the side of the angels. Even if your employer is no angel, it deserves to have its bills paid. The advice in the latter part of this chapter should help you and boost your confidence.

There may be things that you can do to make yourself feel in control. Some people find that it helps to make a call standing up. Why not? The person receiving it will not know. It may also help to remember truisms or to have them on your desk. Examples are:

WE ARE NOT A BANK

> **WE ARE NOT A BRANCH OF THE SAMARITANS**

> **THERE IS NO PROFIT UNTIL**
> **THE MONEY IS IN THE BANK**

Preparation for the call

The following list is asking rather a lot, but it will help
enormously if you make a call armed with the following
information:

- the total amount owing
- month-by-month figures showing how much is
  overdue
- a list of the invoices making up these figures
- information about any queries or unresolved
  disputes
- information about the account's history
- details of any promises made but not kept – this
  means amounts promised, dates and names

Of course, if there are any queries, your call will be more
likely to succeed if you are able to give the answers.

The customer will respect a caller who has all the facts at
his fingertips and makes a request in a firm but friendly
and business-like manner. If you are ill-prepared and have
got the facts wrong, it does not make a good impression.

How to reach the right person

This poses the question 'Who is the right person?' You should not have too many preconceived ideas about this. The right person is the person who is most likely to arrange the payment that you want. It may be the finance director or it may be the most junior office clerk. It does not matter so long as the payment is arranged.

You will be in a strong position if you know the right people in the customer's business, and it is even better if you are on friendly terms with them. In these circumstances, you will ask for someone by name. If this is not the case, there is nothing wrong in asking for advice from the customer's switchboard. You should just say that you would like to discuss an account, and could you please be put through to the right person. It is not good practice to berate an unfortunate switchboard operator about an overdue payment.

It is also sound practice to ask for a named position such as accounts payable manager. It is reasonable to ask for a medium level of authority such as this. You may be directed to a more junior person, but this does not matter so long as you get the help that you need. If you are fobbed off or cannot get a fair response, you should ask to speak to a senior person.

Many customers are reasonable for much of the time, and you will often succeed in getting through to the right person. Getting satisfaction when you have done so may be another matter. There are four possible reasons for not being able to speak to the right person. In ascending order of seriousness, they are:

- He is (for a short time) out or busy
- He is (for a long time) out or busy
- He is (for a short time) deliberately avoiding you
- He is (for a long time) deliberately avoiding you

It may not be easy to tell which of the above is the case, and you will have to persist in order to find out.

One obvious ploy is to ask to speak to a different person. In many companies, accounts payable are handled by a team, and there should be someone else able to help you. If there is not, you are entitled to be suspicious, though it may in fact be true that only one person is able to deal with the account.

In all cases, you must be persistent and ring again. If necessary, you must ring again and again. If the person you wish to speak to is for a short time avoiding you, out or busy, you will fairly soon be able to hold your conversation. If it is one of the other two cases, you may have to badger the unfortunate switchboard staff. In the end, they may decide that it is less trouble to put you through than to keep taking your calls.

Humour, as always, may open doors. You could try something like 'I am the Chief Executive of the National Lottery, and he has won 10 billion pounds. I want to arrange for Joan Collins to present the cheque. Please, please will you put me through?' You will nearly always get through eventually, but not always. If you are ultimately forced to admit failure, you should leave an unmistakable message and follow it up with a letter. You must then consider your next step, which may be some form of sanction, perhaps legal action.

A successful call

What is a successful call? It is, of course, one that results in
a payment being received shortly afterwards. This is the
overwhelming objective, but there are other aims as well.
You should probably try to achieve the following:

- get the maximum possible payment in the minimum
  possible time
- make progress in resolving any disputes or queries
- find out more about your customer, and build up your
  database for future reference
- maintain and improve your relationship with the customer

It pays to adopt a friendly attitude for most of the time. This
is not only good for your blood pressure, it is also the most
effective way of dealing with most customers. Try to get on
friendly terms with the person at the other end of the line
and perhaps find out some personal details. This may help
next time. It is an extremely good opening to say 'Happy
Birthday' or 'How much did the sponsored walk raise?'
Much of the human race is quite nice, rather like you in fact.

This does not mean that you should let anyone take liberties or treat you badly. You should be fair, friendly and firm. Sometimes, firmness has to be the priority. You should aim to be respected, which is not a contradiction with being liked. You will certainly know people who are well-liked as well as respected, and this is what you should try to achieve.

You should try to sound confident. You may think that this is not very helpful advice and as much use as being told to be happy. Either you are or you are not. The distinction is that you are advised to *sound* confident rather than be confident. A perceived lack of confidence is distinctly unhelpful and will not be respected by the person whom you are calling. So try to sound confident, even if you are not. It will help if you have prepared thoroughly, believe in what you are doing and have read this chapter carefully.

The intelligent use of questions should be part of your technique. The usual reason for asking a question is a wish to know the answer, and you should ask questions of this sort. A good example is 'When will we receive the payment please?' Another reason for asking questions is to guide the other person towards a certain conclusion. These questions are often put in a set, and you may already know the answers. An example of such a set of questions is:

- Has Mrs Green signed off the invoice now?
- Did you get it in the system before the close-off?
- Is your payment day tomorrow?
- Can I expect the cheque by Monday?

You should ask for a precise amount. The customer may use phrases such as 'I'll let you have something' or 'I'll see what I can do.' This is not good enough, and you should press to know the precise amount. What he can do may only be a very small payment on account, and this might not be acceptable.

The advantage of a telephone call is that it is a conversation, and you should seek to maximise the benefits of this. Seek to engage the other person in a genuine, two-way conversation. It is easy to go on to autopilot and sound as if you are reading from a script. It is easy to fall into this trap, especially if you make a lot of calls. But it is a bad mistake, even if it is a good script. The biggest benefit of a telephone call is that you are speaking to a person. So do not be impersonal.

This section could well be the most valuable in the entire book, so it is worth repeating the key points in the form of a checklist. You might like to tick each point.

- The first priority is to get swift payment
- There are other objectives as well
- It pays to be friendly most of the time
- It often pays to get on personal terms
- Do not let anyone take liberties
- Be persistent
- Aim to be both liked and respected
- Try to sound confident
- Use questions intelligently
- Ask for a precise amount
- Make it a genuine two-way conversation
- Do not sound as though you are speaking from a script

The conclusion

At the conclusion of the call, you should both know exactly what is going to happen next. Ideally, a prompt payment is going to be what happens next. If so, you should both know the amount, the date and the method of payment. Just possibly, nothing at all is going to happen next. If so, you should both know it. You should try not to end the call in an inconclusive way.

One of you should sum up by saying what is going to happen. If possible, it should be the customer who says it. This is because he is more likely to feel committed, and because there is less chance of a misunderstanding. If you cannot get him to do it, then you must do it yourself, perhaps prefaced by a remark such as 'I am making a note that you said that.' Whatever happens, it must be clear.

Summary

If you can use the telephone effectively, you will be a good way towards being proficient at credit control. If you have a lot of accounts, it will be necessary to operate according to a system of priorities. It is not usually a good idea to start at A and work through to Z.

Today we have:

- seen the advantages and disadvantages of telephone collection
- studied the right attitude
- seen how to prepare for a call and reach the right person
- most importantly, looked at several of the features of a successful call
- seen how to conclude the call and what to do afterwards

Dealing with excuses

If you have any experience at all of credit control, you will have encountered numerous excuses. They range from the plausible to the incredible, and from almost a good reason for not paying through to downright lies and semi-fraud. Be very, very sceptical, but do not overlook the possibility that you are hearing the truth. It happens very rarely, but dogs actually have been known to eat cheques.

There are millions of excuses, and more are invented every day. They are best examined in groups, with some general advice considered first. So, today's programme is as follows:

- The right approach
- Problems with the customer's system
- Problems with the paperwork
- Disputed terms
- The customer says he is short of money
- Other excuses

The right approach

You will probably not want to call your customer a liar, even if he is, you know it and he knows that you know it. Fortunately, virtually all excuses can be overcome without resorting to this. It is probably all right to allow a note of slight scepticism to appear in your voice, whilst at the same time promising vigorous cooperation to overcome the desperately unfortunate set of circumstances that you both so much regret. For example, you might promise to fax a copy of a missing invoice within 60 seconds so that he will have a whole afternoon to prepare a cheque and catch the post.

You should be firm when confronted with an excuse. Not calling your customer a liar is not the same as letting him get away with it. You should firmly resolve to overcome the excuse and get payment in the near future. Your tone of voice and attitude to the customer should convey this resolve. Humour may sometimes be effective.

You should act quickly to do what is necessary. It is probable that by the time you hear an excuse, payment has already been held up. Do not permit any more delay. Whatever you decide to say and do, you should say and do it quickly.

You should most definitely then keep an eye on the situation and take action if payment still is not made. Once action has been taken to overcome a problem, there should be no excuse for continued non-payment. You should not agree to wait for a routine payment date (such as once a month) but should press for an immediate special payment. If you do not get it, you will have to consider some firm action.

You may have to be prepared to take trouble and time to help the customer overcome the problem. This may be infuriating because it is probably not your fault and the customer may even be telling lies. But you want to get paid, and the work may have to be done.

These rules can be simply summed up as follows:

* Be firm
* Act quickly
* Follow up quickly, and act decisively if necessary
* Humour can be effective
* Be prepared to spend time on the matter

Problems with the customer's system

Examples of this are:

* no-one to sign the cheque
* invoice not approved
* computer problems
* account not reconciled
* records with the accountant

By definition, the problem is the customer's fault and not yours. You are therefore fully justified in taking a firm line in demanding that the customer sort it out and get payment to you. You are entitled to be sceptical, and you may have to embarrass the customer if necessary. Be persistent.

A good first step is to isolate the problem and press for immediate payment of unaffected invoices. This is a good first step with other types of problem too. It will not help in cases such as the alleged absence of a person to sign a cheque. However, in the case of unapproved invoices, you should very strongly resist an attempt to hold up payment of other invoices that are approved.

The next step is to give what help you can to get the problem solved. For example, in the case of an unapproved invoice, you might fax proof of delivery or resolve a price query. If an account is not reconciled, you might send copies of statements and other details. You should be insistent in giving help, even if it is not especially wanted. Your payment is being held up, and the customer is getting help with a problem. So he should be pleased.

Some problems will be beyond your help and must be solved by the customer. You should take a strong line, perhaps use humour and perhaps embarrass the customer. Most problems can be overcome if the will is there. The human race managed to send cheques before computers were invented. If there are computer problems, you should say that a handwritten cheque is completely acceptable. If the records are with the accountant, suggest that they be brought back. Or you might say that you will take a payment on account for 98 per cent of the statement balance, with the rest to follow next week.

You are entitled to be very sceptical indeed when you are told that there is no-one available to sign cheques. This is almost always untrue. Provision for emergencies is virtually always made. You might try asking if they plan to pay the wages this week. Or you could ask what would happen if the telephone were to be cut off. You should listen to the answer and then say that the telephone is safe, so could you have that cheque instead?

Problems with the paperwork

Examples of this are:

- missing invoice
- incomplete details on the invoice
- delivery address not specified
- no order number

Some of these problems may be the fault of the customer, and some may be the fault of the supplier. In some cases, there may be faults on both sides. Trying to pin the blame does not normally help much, so it is best to offer cooperation in solving the problem. As always, a good first step is to isolate the problem and press for payment of the remainder of the account.

By far the most common excuse is an allegedly missing invoice. This must rank with 'the cheque is in the post' as the most frequent subterfuge. The obvious response is to provide a copy as quickly as possible. This should be done by fax or other electronic means (if available), and a hard copy should be sent by post in confirmation. You should then ring to check that the copy has been received and will be paid quickly. The customer should not be allowed to get away with any further delay.

You may notice that a customer repeatedly calls for copy invoices and that this regularly delays payment. You might try ringing ahead of the due payment date and asking if copy invoices are required this month. You could say that you will send them now so that he will be able to make payment on the due date. The customer should soon realise that the trick has been discovered and is not worth repeating.

It is also very common for a customer to refuse payment until a valid order number is quoted. This is especially true of large companies, and order numbers often seem to be more important to accounts department staff than to anyone else in the organisation. It can sometimes be difficult to get an order number when an order is placed, and even more difficult to get one after an order has been fulfilled.

Having said this, you must obtain an order number and provide it. The person who placed the order must be asked, and if necessary he should be asked very firmly indeed. The law will very probably be on your side, but this will be an abstract point. You must get the order number. For the future, your own staff may need to be told that orders from this particular customer should only be processed when an order number is provided.

There are many other examples of problems with the paperwork that may be used as an excuse to delay payment. The answer is to cooperate in obtaining and supplying the missing information.

Sometimes it will be easy to get the missing information, but sometimes it will be hard. It may be necessary to take a firm line with a customer who is making unreasonable demands and will not help in solving a problem. 'Take a firm line' is easy to say but may not be easy in practice. There may occasionally be no alternative to sanctions, such as legal action or refusing future orders. It can be helpful to bring in a more senior level of management, on either side or on both sides.

It is often very reasonable to ask for a large payment on account whilst problems are being resolved. If the monthly payment is always slightly over £10,000, you might, for example, ask for £10,000 with a small cheque to follow later. If necessary, a senior manager might be brought in to make this request.

Disputed terms

It must be clear that there are two very different sets of
circumstances that are covered by the phrase 'disputed
terms':

1 the customer will not accept the terms that have been
   agreed
2 the customer will not accept your terms, and never did
   agree them.

It is debatable whether or not the first set of circumstances
should really be called a dispute. Wilful non-payment
might be a better description. But if one side says that there
is a dispute, then there is a dispute, and you must decide
what to do.

Your first step must be to point out the terms that have
been agreed, and if necessary prove that they have been
agreed. Hopefully, you can do this, and you may, for
example, need to send a photocopy of a signed order that
referred to the terms. The next step is to ask the customer
why they are refusing to honour the agreement. If it turns
nasty, you might ask how they would react if you did not
honour your side of the agreement, perhaps by putting up
the price or by unloading the delivery lorry half a mile
short of the factory gate. These are embarrassing questions
and difficult to answer. If it really is a clear-cut agreement,
the only truthful answer is that they are operating a
dishonest policy. You are most unlikely to hear these words.
Instead, you will probably be given weasel phrases about
restructuring company procedures or similar nonsense. It is
possible they will say that although a document has been

signed, its significance was not appreciated and no moral commitment was made.

You are (presumably) in the right, both legally and morally. For all that, you have a practical decision to make and probably do not want to lose a customer. You may decide to take legal action to enforce your rights, but probably you will not. Apart from anything else, the customer will probably have paid before this can be done. More practically, you may take other action such as suspending further deliveries or withdrawing cooperation on a contract.

You might decide to give in or to try and negotiate a compromise. If you do this, you must hold them to the absolute letter of the revised agreement. They must not be allowed to break this agreement as well. Whatever the outcome, you will have to take a policy decision about future orders. There must be a clear commitment that the terms (whatever they are) for future business are binding on both sides.

The situation is completely different if the terms were never properly agreed in the first place. You should ask yourself why this was not done and realise that this time you may not be legally and morally in the right. In this case, you are on weak ground, and your skills of persuasion are needed. You must try to show that your terms are fair, reasonable, generally accepted in the industry and so on. You might point out that in Britain statutory interest applies in some circumstances. This is being introduced in stages, but, in the absence of a contrary agreement, interest often applies after 30 days. Statutory interest is explained in detail tomorrow.

You must try to negotiate with the customer, and
unfortunately you will not be doing so from a position of
strength. If you make concessions, ensure that the customer
honours the new agreement. Ask immediately and ask
insistently when the new date arrives. Also, you must
decide a policy for future business. It is up to you to agree
the terms for this and then ask the customer to honour the
agreement.

The customer says he is short of money

You are not likely to hear a customer say that he is short of
money, and even less likely to hear that payment cannot be
made because he does not have sufficient funds. You are
more likely to hear weasel phrases such as 'temporary
liquidity imbalance' or 'cash-flow disequilibrium'. Such
phrases can mean one of the following:

* The customer is lying and can pay if he wants to
* The customer is having problems and finds it
  inconvenient to pay now, but can do so if he has to
* It really is impossible for the customer to pay now

Needless to say, it can be difficult to know exactly what is
the true position. However, whatever the exact situation,
you are legally and morally in the right. You have fulfilled
your side of the bargain and the customer has not.

It is normally wise to be sceptical about an inability to pay.
A customer usually can pay if he has to, perhaps with
difficulty and perhaps at the expense of putting off another
payment. It is quite often a competitive situation, and the
supplier who applies the most pressure may be the one

TEMPORARY LIQUIDITY
IMBALANCE, HONESTLY...

who is paid first. You should be aware of this, and perhaps you should decide that you will be the supplier who applies the most pressure. After all, the electricity bill is almost certain to be paid. There is a reason for this and it is that the sanction of disconnection is genuinely feared.

It is as well to be aware of the law relating to wrongful trading by a company. Part of it may be summarised as: 'Directors may be disqualified and be personally liable for debts if they carry on trading when they know, or ought to know, that there is no reasonable prospect of avoiding insolvent liquidation.' If you are told that payment cannot be made now, you should insist on speaking to a senior person, and you should make sure that he understands the seriousness of the position. You are very unlikely to be told that you will never be paid. If this is said, you are facing liquidation or insolvency and a possible bad debt. Instead you are likely to be told that you will be paid at some time in the future, and you are likely to be asked to be patient. If you are a regular supplier, you may be asked to maintain supplies during the difficult period. Your reaction will partly depend on your knowledge of the customer and the details of the proposals that you will be given. You should ask for as much detail as you consider necessary and reasonable, and then exercise your judgment. Some customers do have a bad patch, come through it and deserve support. Other customers are flawed and have problem after problem after problem.

Needless to say, if you do agree to support a customer, you should continue to monitor the situation very closely. It is a very good idea to ask the customer to let you have post-dated cheques in support of the proposal that he makes. This idea is likely to be resisted, but it is a very reasonable request and an indication of the customer's confidence and good faith. If the customer does not have enough confidence to give post-dated cheques, why should you have the confidence to support him?

Other excuses

These are divided into three sections:

1 The cheque is in the post.
2 It's already been paid.
3 There is a technical fault with the cheque.

The first of these has achieved that status of a national joke. You will certainly have heard it numerous times. It is very unfair on the postal authorities, which do not usually deserve the blame that they are given. Very occasionally, a cheque has been delayed, but more often a lie has been told. The person giving the excuse may sometimes sincerely believe it but not be aware that a colleague has failed to sign or post the cheque. 'In the post' often means 'In an envelope in the drawer'.

It is a complete waste of time to ask for the cheque number because the information is of no use even if supplied. The standard response is to wait for a very small number of days and then ask for a duplicate to be sent. You should say that the original cheque will be returned, or that it can be stopped. The customer may want to allow more time for the cheque to arrive, but this should be strongly resisted.

You should insistently ask for the duplicate payment to be sent very quickly. If it is a large or important payment, you should ask for a bank transfer instead of a cheque. If a second payment is delayed, you are entitled to be very cross and consider what sanctions need to be taken.

You are advised to proceed with caution when you hear the words 'Already paid'. It may be true, or at the very least the person saying it may believe it to be true. Mistakes do get made, and perhaps one has been made by you or one of your colleagues.

The best approach is a friendly offer to cooperate with the customer in getting to the root of the problem. In most cases you will not be able to solve it by yourself, and a pooling of information is essential. Of course, if the customer will not cooperate, you should be suspicious and do what checks you can in the circumstances. The problem is that you may be looking for something that is not there. If the customer will not cooperate, and if you cannot find anything yourself, firm action on your part is almost inevitable. This will force the customer to produce the details if they exist.

The best clue is often to get the customer to tell you the date that the cheque was debited to his bank account. This may well result in the discovery that it has never actually been debited to his bank account. If it has been debited, the date may differ significantly from the date that he said it was paid. From the date that the bank account was debited, you should be able to work out the date when the cheque must have been banked. You should then check your own banking and allocations for that day very thoroughly. However, even this is not foolproof, because the cheque could have been banked by someone else.

The three most common technical faults with cheques are:

1 Not signed.
2 The words and figures differ.
3 Post-dated.

It may be a mistake on the customer's part, but it is sometimes done deliberately in order to gain extra time. You may spot the error yourself or you may only find out when the cheque is rejected by the customer's bank.

The normal response is to send or take the cheque back to the customer and get him to alter or replace the cheque. If you do this, it should be done very quickly, and you should press for a speedy response from the customer. There should be no excuse for a delay in returning the corrected cheque to you.

There is another way and it is a way that is highly recommended, though it can normally only be done if you spot the error before the cheque has been banked. You can photocopy the cheque and then bank it anyway, despite the error. Banks do not scrutinise cheques in the way that once was normal practice. So there is a good chance that the cheque will be accepted, and if the amount of the cheque is not large, there is a reasonable chance that it will be paid as well.

When the cheque has been banked, you should ring the customer and say that you have noticed the unfortunate error on the cheque. He can hardly say that it was done deliberately and is bound to apologise. It could, of course, have been a genuine mistake anyway. You should then tell the customer that you have banked the cheque and ask him to ring his bank to request that the cheque be paid when it arrives. Banks will normally respond to a telephone request such as this, though they may want written confirmation. The customer will find it impossible to give a good reason for not doing what is asked. If he will not do it, you will know that it was deliberate and must accordingly take a very firm line.

Summary

Dealing with excuses is a big subject and an important skill to master. Today we have:

- studied general guidelines for an effective response
- looked in detail at many of the common excuses
- examined the standard reactions
- looked at some unusual and imaginative counterploys

Tomorrow starts with an interesting set of questions so that you can test what you have learned in the past four days. We will then look at further collection methods and also at when interest can be charged.

Other collection methods and interest

Letters and telephone calls are the two most common methods of collection, and there are good reasons for this. They are practical and they work. But they are not the only methods, and other ways can be very useful. Today we will look at some of these other ways, and we will study the very important topic of how you might get interest on a late payment. A new law in Britain provides for statutory interest, and this will take effect in stages.

Before this, we will mark passing the week's halfway point by testing your understanding of what has been covered in the first four days. In honour of the radio programme, this section is called 'Twenty Questions'. Today's complete programme is as follows:

- Twenty Questions
- Credit agencies
- Personal visits
- Factoring
- Interest

Twenty Questions

Credit control is an art as well as a science. Consequently, only a few of the questions have answers that are absolutely right or absolutely wrong. You should note that Question 3 below comes into this category. Most are a matter of opinion, though some opinions are more valuable than other opinions. The 20 questions cover many of the points that we have considered in the first four days this

week. The answers are at the end of the book, but you should jot down your thoughts before checking them. If you agree on 15 or more, you will have done well.

1   Name three things that should be achieved when a new account is opened.
2   You should aim for the 3 Fs when a new account is opened. What are the 3 Fs?
3   Does printing the payment period on an invoice make that period legally enforceable?
4   What should you do if you receive no reply to a request for a reference?
5   When must conditions of sale be agreed in order to be legally binding?
6   Name three advantages of standard letters.
7   Name two disadvantages of standard letters.
8   Name five features of a good standard letter.

9 What proportion of good final warning letters achieve early payment?
10 Name four features of a good final warning letter.
11 What is the main advantage of telephone collection?
12 What is the main disadvantage of telephone collection?
13 Name four pieces of information that it is helpful to have when making a telephone call.
14 Name seven key points for making a successful call.
15 What should you do immediately after a call?
16 Name an excuse that should cause you to proceed with caution.
17 What is a good first step when dealing with most excuses?
18 How would you respond to the excuse of 'computer failure'?
19 How would you deal with repeated requests for copy invoices, month after month?
20 What should you do if you notice a technical fault on a cheque?

Credit agencies

The many services that credit agencies provide for the credit controller may be grouped into two categories:

1 provision of information
2 assistance with collection.

Sources of information are covered tomorrow, and the role of credit agencies in providing information is left until then. Today we will consider the role of credit agencies in assisting with collection.

There are a large number of credit agencies, and the
services that they provide vary widely. Some specialise in
particular trades or particular geographic areas. Some –
Dun and Bradstreet is a well-known example – offer a very
wide range of services and cover all areas. Credit agents
will completely take over the collection of debts and do
what is necessary in order to obtain payment. The precise
arrangements and the methods used will be a matter of
individual negotiation, but typically will be based on the
sending of standard letters. Telephone calls may be made as
necessary. Fees may be negotiated according to the services
provided, and payment is often in the form of a percentage
of the debts collected.

An obvious advantage of passing debts to a credit agency is
that it can save work. Credit agencies prosper because they
are good at the job, so you are likely to get an efficient
collection service. Some people wish to distance themselves
from the appearance of putting pressure on a customer, and
by appointing a credit agent they think that they get the
best of both worlds. Pressure is applied, which suits them,
but they feel that the customer will blame the credit agent
rather than themselves.

Credit agencies claim that the mere involvement of a third
party increases the pressure. Customers are likely to believe
that a supplier is serious about credit control. They are likely
to respect the agency as professionals unlikely to be swayed
by excuses. Of course, they would say that, wouldn't they?
But there is probably some truth in the belief.

Nothing is for nothing, and the service has to be paid for.
Some credit controllers do not want to pay for something

that they can do themselves. Disputes, queries and mistakes on an account can greatly hamper collection by an agency. Queries will probably have to be referred back and can slow things down and severely hamper the collection effort. The involvement of an agency can sometimes be the catalyst that forces a supplier to sort out its systems and improve the standard of its sales ledger.

Credit agents are particularly suited to the collection of debts by means of the legal process. Many have specialist departments to handle this work, and in doing so they are rivals to firms of solicitors. Indeed, many employ solicitors. Again, they often negotiate a fee based on a percentage of the sum recovered.

A final warning letter from a credit agent does carry a lot of weight, and in this it is similar to a final warning letter from a solicitor. Credit agents handle a large number of legal collections and have efficient systems to support their actions.

Finally, it is worth mentioning that some agents will provide a variety of other services, including purchase of debts, monitoring non-payers, and bailiff services. Some agents will assist with international collections.

Personal visits

Personal visits are an extremely expensive method of collection. For this reason, it pays to be very selective and to plan each visit carefully. However, they are very effective and are usually regarded as the most successful collection method of all. The human contact is the principal reason for this. It is like a telephone call, but even better. It is possible to look the other person in the eye, and he will then feel under pressure to play fair and make a payment. Excuses are more difficult to make. After all, if the managing director is in the next office, it cannot be said that there is no-one to sign the cheque.

It is usually best to give advance notice of a visit. This gives the customer a chance to prepare any matters that he would like to discuss and to get a cheque ready for you to take away. You should normally give advance notice of anything that you would like to discuss, and specify the amount of the cheque that is due and that you would like to take away with you. This all sounds very formal but it can normally be a friendly occasion.

Personal visits are so effective that you should take every opportunity that occurs. If you are driving past the end of the road, it may pay to take the time to make a visit. When a salesman or other employee is due to make a visit, it may pay to ask for a cheque to be made available for collection. This need not involve negotiating, and it has some of the advantages of a full visit.

Factoring

Factoring has considerable advantages, but at a cost. The factoring company will pay up to about 85 per cent of the amount of each approved invoice shortly after they are issued, and will then take over the collection of the debts. When it has been paid, it will deduct interest and its agreed fee and pass the remaining sum to the supplier.

The early release of cash is usually the principal attraction of factoring, and it is a source of finance for a business that may be short of working capital. It is not as expensive as is often supposed, but it does of course have a cost. The factoring company will take as its fee an agreed percentage of the sums advanced, plus interest for the period until it is paid.

Factoring companies are generally large and efficient, and they will operate routine credit-control procedures to collect the money. These typically involve sending standard letters, with telephone follow-up in appropriate cases. They tend to operate in a remorseless way, which suits many of their clients. They will proceed through the letters to a final warning letter and then to legal action.

Like credit agencies, they are sometimes respected because they are third parties and because they are not easily swayed by special pleading. Also like credit agencies, they can suffer because they are an extra link in the chain. Queries and disputes have to be referred back to the client.

Factoring is usually disclosed to the customer but sometimes it is not disclosed. When it is disclosed, the customer is asked to pay directly to the factoring company. When it is not disclosed, the customer pays the supplier, who passes it on to the factoring company.

Sometimes, factoring is with recourse and sometimes it is without recourse. If it is without recourse, the factoring company takes the bad debt risk on approved invoices that it has accepted. This is a big benefit, and there is of course an appropriately higher fee. If the factoring is with recourse, the advance must be repaid to the factoring company if the customer has not paid within a specified period.

Interest

In Britain, a customer may be forced to pay interest on late payment if one of the following three circumstances apply:

1 in many cases, if legal action has been taken and judgment obtained;
2 if provision is made for it in a contract;
3 if statutory interest applies.

These circumstances are very different, so we will look at each one in turn.

If legal action has been taken and judgment obtained
If an action is brought in a county court, interest at the statutory rate may be claimed from the date of the issue of the summons to the date of judgment, or of payment if earlier. Interest continues to run in some cases. Interest also applies if judgment is obtained in the High Court.

If provision is made for it in a contract
It has always been free to both parties to a contract to agree that interest will be payable in the event of late payment. Provided that such interest provides a 'substantial remedy', it takes precedence over statutory interest. It is up to supplier and customer to negotiate the agreed terms.

If statutory interest applies
Many countries have a law that provides for interest to be paid in the event of late payment, though in many cases the law is not particularly effective. Until recently, Britain did not have such a law, but we now have The Late Payment of Commercial Debts (Interest) Act 1998. It only applies to commercial debts and excludes consumer credit, hire purchase, mortgages etc. The new Act takes effect in three stages:

1 contracts made from 1 November 1998 – small
   businesses against large businesses and the public
   sector;
2 contracts made from 1 November 2000 – small
   businesses against all businesses and the public sector;
3 contracts made from 1 November 2002 – all businesses
   and the public sector against all businesses and the
   public sector.

A small business is one with 50 or fewer employees
(averaged over a year) and with part-time employees
counting pro rata. It is felt that small businesses are
particularly vulnerable to the sin of late payment, and so
they have been given a four-year advantage period.

The Act states that if a contract specifies a payment period,
that payment period will apply so long as it is reasonable.
If this is not the case, custom and practice may apply, but
stern tests will be made. The onus is on the customer to
show that it is reasonable. Failing this, it will be deemed to
be 30 days. The 30 days run from the later of the supply of
goods or services and the giving of notice of a required
payment (usually by sending an invoice).

The Act also states that if a contract specifies a rate of
interest, that rate of interest will normally apply. But the
contractual rate of interest must give a 'substantial remedy'.
If it does not do so, or if there is no agreement at all, the
rate of interest will be '8 per cent over base rate'. This is a
high rate and enough to be a real deterrent. In the absence
of an agreement on interest and the payment period, it is 8
per cent over base starting on day 31.

Statutory interest does not have to be claimed at once, and a claim may be made at any time until it is statute-barred. This is five years in Scotland and six years in the rest of the UK. A liquidator or administrator may make a claim within these periods, as well as the business itself.

This is very significant in cases where payment is late, but a supplier does not claim statutory interest for fear of annoying a customer. If the relationship subsequently goes sour, the supplier can resurrect the matter and make a claim. A lot of slow payers are going to get a nasty shock in the coming years.

The supplier may make a claim for statutory interest by notifying the purchaser that a claim is being made. It is recommended that this be done in writing and that the purchaser be given full details of the claim, including invoice numbers, dates, amounts etc. The purchaser should also be given the daily interest rate. If there is a dispute that cannot be settled, or if the purchaser just does not pay the interest, the supplier may commence a legal action. If there is an unresolved dispute, the court will decide.

A business that is paid late has the option of making a claim for interest under the Act. In practice, many businesses do not do so, the main reason being that they do not wish to upset their customers. This has to be an individual decision, but you should be aware of statutory interest and your rights. You should also be aware that you may make a claim after a considerable time has elapsed.

Interest is a big and important subject. We will close with a checklist of some of the key points.

- Interest may be claimed if a legal action is successful
- Provision for interest can by agreement be included in a contract
- The law on statutory interest takes effect in three stages
- Until 1st November 2002, only small businesses can claim statutory interest
- Unless a contract or custom and practice says differently, statutory interest starts after 30 days
- Unless a contract says differently, the rate for statutory interest is 'base plus 8 per cent'
- If a customer refuses to pay statutory interest, legal action may be taken
- Statutory interest may be claimed until the matter is statute-barred

Summary

We started today with 20 questions to make sure that the topics covered in the first four days have been well understood. After that, we have:

- looked at the important services provided by credit agencies
- seen how to get the best value out of personal visits
- looked at the services offered by factoring companies
- seen how we might receive interest and, in particular, studied the law on statutory interest

Sources of information and signs of trouble

Good information is one of the pillars of good credit management, and it is the means of ensuring that the right decisions are made. Today we look at sources of good information and at how it may be obtained. Signs of trouble too are extremely important. We will look at the common indications and see when you should be put on guard. Today's full programme is as follows:

- Credit agencies
- Trade references
- Bank references
- Companies House
- Trade sources
- Your own records
- Signs of trouble

Credit agencies

It was explained yesterday that credit agencies assist in collection or even take over collection. This aspect of their work has already been covered, and today we will look at their role as providers of information.

Some credit agencies specialise in certain areas or industries, whereas others aim to provide a service in all areas. Intrum Justita and Dun and Bradstreet are two well-known examples of the latter, and you are more likely to encounter larger agencies such as these. You should always treat their opinions with respect, but do remember that they are not infallible.

Credit agencies sometimes have to operate with incomplete
information, and this can lead to what some users feel is
excessive caution. This is an understandable response, and
it should be remembered that later events sometimes prove
that the caution was justified.

The most common time to use the services of an agency is
when a new account is opened. It may also be a good idea
to do so if an unsatisfactory reference is received or if there
is some other cause for concern. It can be expensive to
regularly check all customers, but it should certainly be
considered for big and important accounts. Especially, it
should be considered when warning signs are detected or
when payment performance is deteriorating. It should also
be considered when there is a big increase in business.

It is traditional to obtain credit opinions and factual
information by post, but fax and on-line access are now
almost universally available. Some agencies offer to sell

their services by means of pre-paid vouchers; one for each enquiry. This can be a good idea, but you should make sure that you do not purchase more services than you will actually need.

Do not forget that you are interested in the speed at which bills are paid as well as the bad debt risk. Some companies, especially big companies, are very safe and very slow. Agency reports may have to be interpreted.

The following are among the services provided by agencies:

- *Company report*: this is usually the most used service. It will give such factual information as incorporation details and the names of directors. It will extract key figures from recent accounts, such as turnover, profit and net working capital. Precise details vary from company to company, but you should get a spread of relevant factual information. Many agencies will include an assessment of how long the company takes to pay its bills. This may be based on published information and on enquiries made. A recommendation for a credit limit may be made.
- *Personal report*: this may be similar to a company report, but it will relate to an individual, a sole trader or a partnership. Obviously, incorporation details are not available, but a search for county court judgements and bankruptcy proceedings should be made.
- *Credit ratings*: these may apply both to companies and to unincorporated bodies. There are many systems, and the ratings awarded by the American company Moodys is a well-known example. Banks in particular highly prize a Moodys Triple A rating. The same principles are applied to businesses and to individuals. Credit ratings are often

included with a company report or a personal report. It should be remembered that a credit rating is an opinion. It is up to you what you do with it.

- *Tracing services*: here, the agent will try to locate an individual or business that cannot be found.
- *Report on directors*: this is a full report on names, addresses, dates of birth, dates of appointment, directorships of other companies etc.

Trade references

These were covered in detail in Sunday's opening chapter, which contains an example of a good letter requesting a trade reference. The manipulation of trade references can always happen, but it is rare, and they often produce very useful results. The taking of trade references is common practice when an account is opened, and it is also possible to do it on a later occasion. Key considerations are as follows:

- It is best to send a pre-printed form that can easily be marked for a reply
- A stamped addressed envelope should be sent
- On no account should a bad reply be ignored
- On no account should the lack of a reply be ignored. It is best to follow up with a telephone call
- It is a good idea to mention a specific sum or to ask what is the highest sum that would be granted for credit
- It may be best to seek a reference from a person selected by yourself, but this may be difficult to achieve

Bank references

In some countries, a request for a bank reference must be made via your own bank, but in Britain this is no longer required, and a direct approach may be made. However, a bank will only provide a reference if it has the written authority of its customer to do so. It is normal to get the customer to sign a form giving the bank permission, and to forward this to the bank together with your request for a reference.

Most banks charge for giving a reference, and £10 to £20 is typical, though it could be more.

Bank references may yield useful information, but many credit controllers find that they are not so useful as trade references. One reason is that a bank will comment on the financial soundness of its customer, but not on its conduct and how quickly it pays its bills. A trade reference may give a more complete picture.

A bank reference is of much more use in preventing bad debts than it is in identifying slow payers who will cause trouble. Of course, early warning of a potential bad debt is extremely valuable and a major reason for taking out a reference. There is usually little point in seeking a bank reference on a large, well-known and respected company. The bank is very likely to say that the company is soundly constructed and good for your figures, but you probably know that anyway. You will not be told if it pays its suppliers promptly.

A bank reference will be given without responsibility and based only on information available to the bank at the time. It is likely to use rather archaic, time-honoured phrases which you will get to recognise in time. Among the favourable phrases, in ascending order of recommendation, are:

* 'We do not think that they would enter into a commitment that they could not see their way clear to fulfil'
* 'Considered good for your figures'
* 'Undoubted'

'Undoubted' is the highest recommendation of all. Among the unfavourable phrases, in ascending order of condemnation, are:

* 'We do not have sufficient information to express a view on this commitment'
* 'We believe that they are fully committed'
* 'We are unable to speak for your figures'

Companies House

All companies registered in Britain are required by law to file certain information at Companies House. This information is available to anyone at all. It only relates to companies and not to individuals, sole traders, partnerships or other bodies, but it is extensive and can be extremely useful.

There are over a million companies registered at Companies House, and each has a unique registered number. It is essential that the correct registered number be quoted when information is sought, and this can be found from a massive index which is kept in alphabetical order. However, a company's registered number must by law be quoted on company stationery and other documents, and this is often a convenient way of locating it.

You can use the services of an agent to get copies of information. A large number of agents are available for this purpose, and it is one of the services offered by many credit agencies. We studied these earlier today. Alternatively, you can get it for yourself. This is not difficult, and Companies House staff are generally very helpful. Application may be made by post, by telephone or in person. On-line access is available (with the necessary equipment).

For companies registered in England and Wales, the Companies House address is in Cardiff. For companies registered in Scotland, it is in Edinburgh. The full addresses are:

Companies House	Companies House
Crown Way	37 Castle Terrace
Maindy	Edinburgh
Cardiff	EH1 2EB
CF4 3UZ	
(Tel: 01222 388 588)	(Tel: 0131 535 5800)

Information may also be obtained from satellite offices located in London, Manchester, Birmingham, Leeds and Glasgow.

Available information includes the following:

- the annual return
- annual accounts
- registered charges on assets
- details of all directors

Other information is always available too. For all but the smallest companies, the annual accounts must be audited.

A private company must file within 10 months of its year-end and a public company must file within 7 months of its year-end. Information about directors must be updated within 14 days of a change occurring.

There can be problems with companies filing late, even though this is an offence for which the directors can be punished. It is quite often companies with problems that file late, and these may be the ones in which you are most interested. Fortunately, Companies House now enforces the requirements more vigorously, and so it is less of a problem than was formerly the case.

Trade sources

Trade sources often include competitors. Some industries have a formal mechanism for an exchange of information, such as a trade association. In many other cases, an information network of contacts is in existence. It is very much in your interests to foster these contacts. You may be competitors, but you can help each other identify and deal with problem payers.

Trade sources very often provide the best source of information of all. It comes from people who are in the same line of business and who know the customer. You may well know the person giving the information and be in a position to return the favour. You will know how reliable the source normally is.

To get the most out of your contacts, it is best not to ask too often, and most definitely you should not use the information to gain an advantage over the person who provided it. You should provide reasonable information when asked yourself, or your source is likely to dry up. There is nothing wrong in exchanging information in this way, but you would not normally disclose the fact to your customer.

This source of information is so valuable that it is worth stressing its importance again. Information here comes from people who really do know, and it is definitely worth forging the necessary links in the trade.

Your own records

Once you have opened an account and traded for a while, your own sales ledger will be a mine of information. It will be so valuable that others, especially the trade sources just mentioned, may well seek information from you. Do not underestimate what is easily and immediately available.

Among other things, your sales ledger will tell you whether or not your customer's payment performance is deteriorating. It will also tell you whether settlement discounts (if available) are being taken.

Signs of trouble

This is a separate section of today's chapter, and it is an extremely important subject. Recognition of the signs of a customer in trouble may enable you to take early action to minimise the damage, and to reduce or eliminate the risk of a bad debt. You may be faced with difficult decisions because nearly all businesses want and need new orders. The last thing that they want is reduced business with an existing customer. Nevertheless, hard choices may have to be made.

Credit control is an art as well as a science. Some of the warning signs may appear as hard evidence, but others may be more difficult to detect. It may be partly a matter of experience and instinct. On no account should you disregard your feelings. Any experienced collector or manager will say that these have sometimes been very useful. You should act on them at least to the extent of making further enquiries, perhaps by consulting a credit agency.

The following are significant warning signs, and you should watch out for them:

- *The customer starts paying more slowly.* This is very often the most important sign of all, and it cannot be hidden. The reason may be a policy decision to pay more slowly, which is bad news for another reason, or it may be a sign of administrative problems. The third possibility is that the customer is having difficulties paying its bills and that it is a case of 'cannot' rather than 'will not'.

Experience shows that virtually every insolvency is preceded by a slowing down in payments. They never, or almost never, come out of a clear blue sky.

- *Round-sum cheques.* This is a very obvious sign of trouble. They may be sent because a customer is having problems reconciling the account, but it is often done because of a shortage of money. You should take and bank the round-sum payments on account, but be aware of the possible problems indicated.

- *Too many mistakes on cheques.* We looked at this in Wednesday's chapter about dealing with excuses. It is often done to buy time, and sometimes to save interest, but usually because money is short.

- *People always unavailable.* Most people dislike telling lies and repeating excuses, especially if it is to a person that they know. Often, rather than do so, they will avoid contact, not return calls, say that they are in a meeting and so on. People can sometimes be genuinely busy, but it is a bad sign nonetheless.

- *Settlement discount not taken.* It is a bad sign if a customer does not take advantage of a worthwhile settlement discount for prompt payment.

- *Warning by a credit agency.* Credit agencies are professionals, and it is their job to keep a close eye on your customers. You pay them to give you their opinions and to warn you of impending problems. We looked at credit agencies earlier today.

- *Accounts filed late, and creative accountancy.* These two things often go together. Business journalists know that good news usually arrives quickly and bad news is often delayed. If accounts are available late, or later than usual, it is a bad sign. Creative accountancy, such as obscure changes in accounting policy, is usually legal but a bad sign.

- *Unsatisfactory accounts.* You should be able to look at the accounts of a limited company. This may be done by using the services of a credit agency, or you can get them from Companies House yourself. You may be able to spot signs of problems from the figures. A major disadvantage is that you are always looking at out-of-date information. A company has either 7 months or 10 months, from the end of its accounting year, to file its accounts at Companies House.

- *Z scores and similar indicators.* Some very clever people have developed modelling systems for predicting business failure. All sorts of information is fed into the model, and weighting factors are applied. It is claimed that the resulting 'score' indicates the financial health of an organisation and can be used to predict future trouble. Some remarkable successes have been claimed, and it is said that almost all the spectacular failures of recent years were, or could have been, predicted in this way. Alas, most of the claims tend to be made retrospectively. The systems are sold commercially.

- *A feeling that something is not quite right.* At the beginning of this section, it was stressed that you should pay due regard to your feelings. If something feels wrong, then perhaps something *is* wrong. You may detect a strained note in the voice of the person speaking to you. You may detect an unusual choice of words that avoids giving a direct answer to a direct question. Things like this can be significant. If you feel that something may be wrong, it may pay to be careful and make enquiries.

Summary

Today we have looked at how you might detect trouble ahead, and we have looked at how you can find out more about your customers. Both parts have been about information. The programme has covered:

- credit agencies
- trade references
- bank references
- Companies House
- trade sources
- your own records
- signs of trouble

Tomorrow, the last day of the week, we will look at what can be done when normal collection methods fail. The subject is legal action.

The end of the line: legal action

During the first six days of this week, we have studied the best ways to avoid problems and to secure swift and sure payment. These methods are tried and tested and they work, but inevitably there will be a few customers who just do not pay in an acceptable period. This is bad, but do not worry too much. It happens to all businesses of any size. You should, though, worry if it happens too often.

When normal credit-control procedures are exhausted and you are convinced that you are in the right, you ultimately face a choice. You can give up and write off the unpaid amount as a bad debt. Alternatively, you can take legal action to enforce the payment that should be yours. Writing off a debt is sometimes the best thing to do, but it should be avoided if possible. Today we look at the alternative, which is to take legal action to enforce payment.

We will end the day with 15 questions to check your knowledge of what has been studied on Thursday, Friday and Saturday. These supplement the 20 questions that were asked after the first four days. The complete programme is as follows:

- Which jurisdiction?
- Considerations prior to deciding on legal action
- The final warning letter
- Who to use and how to pay
- Correct identification of the other party
- The different routes to winning your case
- Enforcing judgment to get actual payment
- Fifteen questions

Which jurisdiction?

This book will be read in several countries, but reference to the legal system relates to the legal system of England and Wales. For this purpose, Scotland is a foreign country. It has many similarities to the English system, but there are some differences. Most of this chapter concerns advice on general principles and applies to almost all countries.

Considerations prior to deciding on legal action

There are some very important points that you should consider before commencing legal proceedings. Among them are the following:

- *Can the customer pay?* There is an old saying that blood cannot be got out of a stone. If the customer really has not got the means to pay, as opposed to choosing not to do so, there is little point in taking legal action. You will win the case but still not get paid, and will have incurred legal costs as well.

- *Costs.* Legal costs will be incurred if an action is taken. There are ways to minimise them, and you may be able to do some of the work yourself, but some costs cannot be avoided. You may succeed in recovering some of them from the customer.

Some solicitors and credit agencies are willing to operate on the basis of 'no win, no fee' and to be paid a percentage of the amount actually recovered. But you will still be liable for court fees and expenses.

You would be well advised to consider the likely amount of costs, the chances of winning, the chances of recovering some costs from the customer, and the amount of the debt. Then you should take a cool decision about whether to proceed or not.

- *The chances of success.* The chances are probably very good if we measure success by winning the case and getting judgment. The overwhelming majority of actions are successful if measured by this yardstick. This is because in most cases there is no real dispute and the case is undefended. Everyone knows that the money is owing; it is just that the customer will not pay. However, if by success we mean winning judgment and getting payment, the chances of success are less.
- *An understanding of the legal system.* It is important to understand that the legal system is there for you to use. It can provide a forum in which you can make things happen, but it will not make things happen for you. There

are a lot of procedures and rules to be followed which you may find frustrating.

Even though you are in the right, and even after you have won your case and got judgment in your favour, the legal system will not act on your behalf. You must fill in the forms, pay the fees (which you will hope to recover from the defendant) and be proactive every step of the way.

- *The importance of acting quickly.* If a customer is in difficulties, it often happens that several suppliers will take legal action at about the same time. It does not follow that all will get a pro-rata share of whatever money is available. The ones that act decisively may get paid in full and others may get nothing.

Money obtained by the methods of enforcement – seizure of assets by a bailiff being one example – goes to the claimants in the order in which they applied for the enforcement action. Company A that applied on Tuesday may get paid in full, while Company B that applied on Wednesday gets nothing.

The final warning letter

We studied this in detail on Monday, and a good example of such a letter is included in that chapter. You should go back to Monday and check the advice given. However, a summary of the key points is given on the next page. A good final warning letter will achieve payment in more than 50 per cent of all cases. So it is worth doing and worth doing well.

Key features of a good final warning letter

- There should, obviously, only be one final warning letter.
- It should be polite, business-like and to the point.
- It should be relatively short.
- The letter should say exactly what will happen if payment is not made by a specified date.
- It is often a good idea to address it to a person not so far involved, with a copy to the original contact. It is often sound to address the letter to the 'Company Secretary'.
- It is a good idea to send the letter by recorded delivery. This may increase the impact.
- The letter should be credible. It should not contain threats which will not be carried out.

Who to use and how to pay

There are three possibilities and we will consider each in turn:

1 Do it yourself

A company bringing an action in the High Court must use the services of a solicitor, but in nearly all other cases you have the option of doing the work yourself. In the great majority of cases, an action is brought in a county court, and here you are always free to act for yourself. This course is most often taken by large businesses that bring a lot of cases. They may employ specially trained staff. However, nearly all readers of this book would be capable of handling relatively simple cases, though they would need to proceed carefully and cautiously. Easy-to-follow and very helpful leaflets are available from all county courts.

The main advantages of doing it yourself are that you stay in control and minimise costs. The main disadvantages are that you will almost certainly be slower than a specialist, might make mistakes and might not be aware of alternative courses of action.

2 *Employ a solicitor*

This has all the advantages of using an expert. You should get a first-rate service, and, once you have given the solicitor the facts and documents, your involvement can be kept to a minimum. This applies to uncontested cases of course, but nearly all cases are uncontested.

This arrangement suits many people who want to use their time doing other things. Many want to hand it to an expert, put it out of their minds, and then (hopefully) bank a cheque at the end. Although most people do adopt this approach, you can keep in touch with your solicitor, make suggestions and even change your instructions.

In matters of debt collection, there are two sorts of solicitor and two methods of charging. One sort of solicitor is not a specialist and does this sort of work alongside all the other things that solicitors do. The other type is a specialist, or a large firm that has a specialist department for debt collection. Both types may well give good service, but the specialists do have certain advantages. They are likely to use computerised systems that generate the right documents on the right dates.

The traditional way for a solicitor to charge is on the basis of time spent and expenses incurred. Others, especially the specialists, may be willing to work for a flat fee or a percentage of the money ultimately recovered. This can be a very good idea, but do beware. Solicitors generally prosper. Think before you sign away a percentage of a large debt where the chances of recovery are very good.

3   *Employ a credit agency*
This should have nearly all the advantages of using a specialist solicitor, and indeed many credit agencies employ specialist solicitors. Credit agencies handle a lot of cases and should give expert advice and service.

Correct identification of the other party

This sounds obvious, but it is surprising how often a mistake is made. The claim must get it exactly right, and the other party must be correctly identified. A mistake can be put right later, but it will cost time and money.

The most common mistake is a failure to realise that you are dealing with a company. You might know your customer as Belinda Jones, and your summons may be taken out against Belinda Jones, but you have a problem if the business is Belinda Jones Fashions of Wigan Ltd. If she misled you, she might be personally liable, but usually the evidence is there and you have to get it right.

A company must, by law, give its full, correct legal name and its registered number on its notepaper and certain other documents. It is a good idea to send a sample to your solicitor or credit agent.

The different routes to winning your case

In this context, 'winning your case' means getting judgment in your favour. This is not usually very difficult because the majority of cases are undefended. There is often no dispute that the money is owing, but it is necessary to bring a case and win judgment in order to get it. But even with an undefended case, it is necessary to fill in the forms correctly and get the formalities right. If you do not do this, you will not win judgment.

Unfortunately, 'winning your case' is not the same thing as actually getting payment. If the customer still does not pay, you must take steps to enforce the judgment. This is covered in the next section of this chapter.

There are whole books on 'winning your case', and space permits only the very briefest of summaries of the different routes available. However, there are basically four different methods. Following is an outline explanation of each. In practice, the vast majority of cases go through a county court and one of the first two of the routes explained.

1 *An action in a county court.* There are approximately 200 county courts in England and Wales. The most common legal method of debt collection is to issue a claim in one of them. The claim will name the defendant and set out brief details of the claim.

The amount involved must be stated. You may also claim reimbursement of court fees and interest from the date that payment was contractually due. The claim must be served on the defendant (usually by post), and the defendant has 14 days from the date of service to state an intention to defend. If he does not do so, you may apply for judgment.

If a defence is entered, and if no settlement is reached, the case will proceed to a hearing before a judge. This hearing will decide whether or not the money is owing, and if you win, judgment will be given.

2 *An action in the small claims court.* The term 'small claims court' has passed into the language, but strictly speaking there is no such thing. Most claims for amounts less than £5,000 are heard in a county court under the small claims procedure. The issue of the claim is the same as for a claim over £5,000. The difference is that the hearing is held more quickly, cheaply and informally. The strict rules of evidence do not apply. If the case is undefended, or if you win a defended case, judgment may be entered.

3 *An action in the High Court.* The High Court does not normally hear claims for less than £15,000. It is more suited to more complex claims.

4   *A winding-up petition or a petition for bankruptcy.*
    Winding-up relates to a company, and bankruptcy relates
    to an individual. Winding-up and bankruptcy are methods
    of enforcement applied if payment is not made after
    judgment has been entered. However, it is possible to
    apply for them without getting judgment first. It puts a lot
    of pressure upon the company or person that owes the
    money.

Enforcing judgment to get actual payment

The customer should pay shortly after you have won
judgment, and quite often this is what happens. You have
then achieved your objective, won the case and got paid.

Unfortunately, this sometimes does not happen. You must
then take some enforcement action to compel payment. All
involve court fees which you may add to the amount
owing to you, but they must be paid whether or not you
succeed in recovering them later.

It is possible to compel the defendant to attend an oral
examination. If the defendant is a company, a director or
other authorised person must attend. At an oral
examination, the defendant must answer questions under
oath about his assets and income. This may help you to
choose the most effective method of enforcement.

Enforcement is a very big subject, and it is only possible to
include the briefest of brief summaries. However, the
following methods of enforcement are available:

OKAY, HAVE THE SWIMMING
POOL AS WELL

- *Seizure of goods.* This is the most used of the enforcement methods, and it is done by a county court bailiff or a High Court sheriff. After a specified period of time, the goods are sold and the proceeds (after fees and expenses) go to the person who obtained judgment and instructed the bailiff or sheriff.
- *Attachment of earnings order.* Here, an employer is instructed to make deductions from an employee's wages and pass them over for the benefit of the person who obtained the order. By definition, this can only apply to an individual in employment. It cannot apply to a company, partnership or self-employed person.
- *Garnishee order.* This enables you to take over the rights in a debt owing to the judgment creditor (the customer who owes you money) by a third party. It can be any debt, but it is most often a bank or building society account in credit. A bank account in credit is a debt owing by the bank.

- *Charging order.* This gives the applicant a registered legal charge over property, stocks and shares etc. The asset charged cannot be sold without the applicant getting first call on the proceeds.
- *Appointment of a receiver.* The court may appoint a receiver to take possession of future income. This may be, for example, income from rents.
- *Winding-up or bankruptcy.* Winding-up relates to a company, whereas bankruptcy relates to an individual. If winding-up or bankruptcy actually takes place, assets are realised and the proceeds are used to pay the creditors pro-rata to the amount of their debts. The judgment creditor that brings the petition does not get priority over the other creditors. Various rules apply, and preferential creditors rank ahead of ordinary creditors.

Fifteen questions

It is now time to test your understanding with some further questions. All are based on what we have studied in the last three days of the week. The answers are at the end of the book after today's summary, but remember that many of the questions do not have a single right or wrong answer: some are a matter of opinion.

1   Name one of the advantages of using a credit agency to collect debts.
2   Name a disadvantage of using a credit agency to collect debts.
3   What is the most effective collection method of all?
4   From what date may large businesses claim statutory interest?
5   At what rate is statutory interest charged?

6 Name a good time to consult a credit agency.
7 Is 'undoubted' a good bank reference?
8 Name a good way to find a company's registered number.
9 What should you do with round-sum cheques on account?
10 Name a sign of trouble that cannot be hidden.
11 Do most actions for debt recovery succeed?
12 What is the most common problem in identifying a defendant?
13 What is the limit for 'The small claims court'?
14 What is the difference between winding-up and bankruptcy?
15 Can an attachment of earnings order be issued against a self-employed plumber?

Summary

If you have checked the answer to Question 11, you will have been encouraged by the fact that most legal actions succeed, although further effort may be necessary to secure actual payment. It is a shame when legal action has to be taken, but sometimes it is essential. We have today studied the basics and seen how to lay the groundwork for success. We have concentrated on the basic principles and practical matters, rather than a legalistic study of the courts and the law.

Answers to twenty questions
(asked on Thursday)

1 a Obtain all the information needed.
   b Make sensible decisions about credit and terms.
   c Agree the terms of business with the customer.
2 Firm, fair and friendly.
3 No.
4 Do something – probably follow up with a telephone call.
5 Before (or at the time that) a contract is made.
6 a They are cheap.
   b Some customers prefer them.
   c It is possible to include a record of complicated information.
7 a Some will be thrown away.
   b There is no human contact.
8 Nine points are listed in a box on page 22.
9 More than half.
10 Six points are listed in a box on page 24.
11 Personal contact is possible.
12 It is relatively time-consuming.
13 Six points are listed in a box on page 33.
14 12 points are listed in a box on page 38.
15 Make a record.
16 'Already paid'.
17 Isolate the problem and press for quick payment of all undisputed invoices.
18 Ask for a manual cheque.
19 Ring before payment is due and ask if any copies are needed this month.
20 a Send it back for alteration and press for a quick return, *or*

b   bank it anyway and then ask the customer to ring the
     bank and authorise payment.

Answers to fifteen questions (asked on Saturday)

1   It puts pressure on the customer.
2   Queries must be referred back, and it is an extra link in
    the chain.
3   It is usually thought to be personal visits.
4   Contracts made from 1 November 2002.
5   8 per cent over base.
6   When a bad trade reference is received.
7   Yes.
8   It must, by law, be shown on company notepaper.
9   Bank them – but realise that they are a sign of probable
    trouble.
10 The customer pays more slowly than was formerly the
    case.
11 Yes – most are undefended. Getting actual payment
    may still be a problem.
12 Failure to realise that a business is really a limited
    company.
13 £5,000.
14 Winding-up happens to a company. Bankruptcy
    happens to a person.
15 No – it can only be issued against an employed person.